The Data Analyst

Roadmap

A Practical Guide to Launching Your Career in Data

Esther C. Anagu

The Data Analyst Roadmap

For permission requests: anaguestherc@gmail.com

ISBN: 978-978-682-285-3

ACKNOWLEDGMENTS

This book has been a journey shaped by conversations, lessons, and the shared experiences of many people. It would not exist without the support and encouragement I received along the way.

First, to every aspiring data analyst who has ever felt lost, overwhelmed, or unsure of where to begin, thank you. Your questions, doubts, and determination inspired every page of this book. Your stories reminded me of why clarity matters. This book is for you.

To my family and friends, thank you for your patience, understanding, and steady encouragement throughout this writing process. On the days when the words did not flow, your support carried me forward.

To my editor and book project consultant, Aisosa Faith Okoro. Thank you for understanding the vision. I appreciate your strategic ideas and attention to detail, which contributed meaningfully to this masterpiece.

And finally, to you, the reader. Thank you for trusting me to guide you. The work ahead will stretch, challenge, and refine you. But if you stay committed, it will open doors you once thought were out of reach.

CONTENTS

Introduction vii

Part 1: The Foundation: Thinking Like an Analyst

1. Your Starting Point: Understanding the Data World 2
2. The Analyst's Mindset: Asking the Right Questions 12

Part 2: The Technical Toolkit: Speaking the Language of Data

3. Your First Toolkit: Mastering Spreadsheets 21
4. SQL: The Lingua Franca of Data 32
5. Data Visualization: From Numbers to Narratives 42
6. Python: Your Analytical Power Tool 51

Part 3: Your Career Launch Kit

7. Building Your Professional Portfolio 63
8. Your Next Project: Strategic Map of Ideas 73
9. Crafting Your Resume & Cover Letter 83

10. Navigating the Job Market: Networking & Interviews 95

11. Your First 90 Days: Thriving as a Data Analyst 105

12. The Responsible Analyst: Data Ethics and Privacy 114

Appendix: Extended Practice Guides 121

INTRODUCTION

If you are holding this book, you are likely feeling a mix of excitement and confusion. You have heard that data is the new oil. You have heard that data analysts are in high demand and that it is a rewarding and future proof career. The possibilities excite you. But at the same time, you feel overwhelmed.

Where do you even begin? Do you need a degree in mathematics? Do you need to learn multiple programming languages before you can apply for a job? Every article and video seems to recommend a different path and a set of "must-know" tools you must master. It's a confusing landscape, and it can make you feel like you're not cut out for this before you even begin.

Pause for a moment and take a deep breath. This book was written for you.

Over the past few years, I have trained and supported thousands of aspiring analysts across Africa and beyond. Through workshops, mentorship, and countless conversations, I have seen the same pattern repeat itself. Bright, capable people with genuine curiosity step into the world of data with enthusiasm, but without structure. They jump from one tutorial to another, collecting fragments of knowledge instead of building a clear path forward. They end up with a collection of half-finished projects and a deep sense of frustration.

It does not have to be that way.

That's why you have this book in your hands. It is not a dense academic textbook. It is not a collection of random tutorials. It is a roadmap. A practical, structured guide designed to take you from absolute beginner to job ready data analyst with a portfolio that proves your ability.

How to Use This Book

This roadmap is designed to be followed in order. Each chapter builds on the previous one, and each technical section ends with a checklist that helps you measure progress.

- **Read the chapters sequentially.** Don't skip ahead, even if a topic seems familiar.

- **Use the checklists.** At the end of each technical chapter, use the checklists to confirm you've understood the core concepts before moving on.

By the end of this book, you will not just have learned new skills; you will have tangible, professional-quality work to show for it. You will have the confidence and the portfolio you need to start applying for jobs.

Your journey from curious beginner to confident practitioner starts now. Let's take the first step together.

Part 1

THE FOUNDATION

Thinking Like an Analyst

1

YOUR STARTING POINT

Understanding the Data World

I have taught auditors, oil and gas professionals, and fresh graduates. Every time I speak to people who are curious about data, I begin at the same place: making sure they truly understand what data analysis is.

This foundation matters. Once you understand what data analysis really means, you will see why it is an indispensable skill in today's world. More importantly, you will understand the valuable role you can play as a data analyst.

1.1 What Is Data Analysis, Really?

Let us set aside complicated definitions for a moment. I like to think of data analysis as the art of **translation.**

On one side, you have raw data. It is messy and overwhelming, filled with numbers, text, and codes. On the other hand, you have decision makers. CEOs, managers, doctors, and marketers. They need clarity so they can make informed choices.

Your job as an analyst is to stand in the middle. You take raw data, clean it, uncover the patterns within it, and translate those patterns into clear language that drives action. You are the bridge between information and insight.

It is a powerful place to be.

1.2 Finding Your Place in the "Data Kitchen"

The world of "data" can seem vast, with all sorts of confusing job titles. So, let's simplify it. I want to give you a mental map of the four main roles you will encounter.

Think of the data ecosystem as a kitchen. Each role has a distinct responsibility, but they work together to produce results. Here are four of the most common roles you will encounter.

1. **The Data Engineer**

This is the person I rely on to build and maintain the entire kitchen. They make sure the pantry is stocked with high-quality ingredients (data) and that all the plumbing (data pipelines) is clean and working perfectly. Without them, the whole operation shuts down. They are the foundation of the entire operation.

> In a Nutshell: A Data Engineer designs, builds, and maintains the systems that collect and prepare large volumes of data. They are the architects of the data infrastructure. They ensure that clean, reliable data is available for others to analyze.

2. **The Data Analyst (You!)**

This is where you come in. You take the beautiful ingredients the engineer has prepared and get to work. You follow the recipe (the business question) to cook up a fantastic meal that reveals what happened in the past and what's happening right now.

> In a Nutshell: A Data Analyst interprets data to identify trends and answer business questions. They clean and analyze data using tools like SQL and Excel, and then communicate their findings to help leaders make informed decisions.

3. **The Business Intelligence (BI) Analyst**

This role is a close cousin to the Data Analyst. They are expert cooks who also have a flair for presentation. They take the finished analysis and "plate" it on beautiful, interactive dashboards so the restaurant owner can see how business is doing with just a glance. They make data accessible to everyone.

> In a Nutshell: A Business Intelligence (BI) Analyst specializes in creating and managing reports and dashboards that track key business metrics. They use data visualization tools like Tableau or Power BI to help organizations monitor their performance in real-time.

4. **The Data Scientist**

The Data Scientist is the experimental head chef, focused on inventing the future. Instead of just analyzing what happened in the past, they build complex statistical models to predict what might happen next. They answer questions like, "Which customers are most likely to leave our service next month?" Their work is often more exploratory and forward-looking.

> In a Nutshell: A Data Scientist applies advanced statistical and machine learning techniques to make predictions. They build predictive models to forecast trends, understand complex behaviors, and uncover future opportunities.

1.3 Which Role Fits Your Personality?

So, you've seen the main players in the data kitchen. Now comes the fun part: figuring out where *you* might fit best. While these roles often overlap, they attract people with slightly different interests. See which of these descriptions resonates with you the most.

Do you love solving puzzles and asking "Why?"

- If you're the kind of person who enjoys digging deep to find the root cause of a problem; who likes investigating and connecting the dots, then the **Data Analyst** path will likely be a great fit. You'll thrive on being the go-to person for explaining complex business trends.

Do you love visual design and clear communication?

- If you have an eye for design and enjoy making complex information beautiful and easy to understand, you should strongly consider the **Business Intelligence (BI) Analyst** path. You will get immense satisfaction from building a dashboard that people love to use every day.

Do you love building things and working with technology?

- If you enjoy the process of constructing systems and making things work efficiently behind the scenes, you might have the mindset of a **Data Engineer**.

Do you love statistics and predicting the future?

- If you're fascinated by probability, forecasting, and using math to model what *might* happen, then you have the seeds of a **Data Scientist**.

Don't worry if multiple descriptions appeal to you! The key takeaway is that there's a place in the data world for different kinds of thinkers.

1.4 Your Experience Is Your Superpower

Now, I want to share the most important piece of advice in this entire book: **your existing experience is not a limitation. It is an advantage.** So many people I talk to think they need to start from scratch, but that's not true.

The most effective analysts are the ones who combine data skills with their passion and knowledge of a specific field. I had my first degree in accounting, and I now leverage that background in my work as a data analyst within the financial sector. That domain knowledge allows me to ask better questions and interpret results more effectively.

Consider your own background.

- Are you an **accountant**? With the skills in this book, you can become a **Financial Analyst**, a person who doesn't just report the numbers but uses them to guide the company's future.
- Do you have a background in **healthcare**? You can become a **Health Informatics Analyst**, using data to improve patient outcomes and operational efficiency.
- Do you love **marketing**? You can become a **Marketing Analyst**, using data to create campaigns that truly connect with people.

Never discount your background. It gives you a level of insight that a generalist analyst can't compete with.

1.5 Everyone Starts Here: The Core Toolkit

Here is the crucial point that should give you a sense of relief: no matter which of these paths excites you, Data Analyst, BI Analyst, or even future Data Scientist, **everyone starts with the same foundational toolkit.**

You don't need to learn five different programming languages right now. You don't need to master complex statistics today. You just need to start with the essentials that every single data professional uses.

That is the purpose of this roadmap. We will begin with spreadsheets, move to SQL, and then learn data visualization. This core toolkit is your non-negotiable first step, and it is the foundation upon which all of those exciting careers are built.

You now have a map of the data landscape. You know the key roles, you know how your own unique experience can be a superpower, and you know the path we are going to take together.

But before we can analyze any data, we have to learn how to *think* about it. The most successful analysts I know don't just have technical skills; they have a specific way of looking at the world. They are curious, skeptical, and they know how to ask brilliant questions.

So, in the next chapter, we're going to pause before touching any tools and forge your most important weapon: **the analyst's mindset.** Let's begin

2

THE ANALYST'S MINDSET

Asking the Right Questions

Welcome to what I believe is the most important chapter in this entire book. Before we ever open a spreadsheet or write a single line of code, we need to talk about the most valuable skill an analyst possesses: **the ability to ask great questions.**

A great tool or a complex algorithm is useless if you're trying to solve the wrong problem. Your real value isn't in knowing how to use Excel; it's in knowing *why* you're using it. This chapter is about building your "analyst's mindset."

2.1 From Vague Problems to Clear Questions

In the real world, problems rarely come in a neat package. You'll get a vague request like:

"Our sales are down."

"We need to improve user engagement."

A junior analyst might just start pulling random sales data, but a great analyst pauses first and thinks. Their job is to act like a detective and turn that vague problem into a specific, answerable question.

Let's see it in action:

Vague Problem: "User engagement on our app is low."

A Great Analyst Asks:

- "What do we *mean* by engagement? Is it daily logins? Is it the time spent on a certain feature? The number of comments made?"
- "Which user group has the lowest engagement? Is it new users from the last 30 days? Users on Android devices?"

The Specific, Answerable Question:

"What is the average number of daily logins for users who signed up in May, compared to users who signed up in April?"

Did you notice the difference?

The first statement is unclear and difficult to act upon. The second is measurable and answerable. You can't solve the first, but you can absolutely answer the second. Your first job is always to be the person who brings this clarity.

2.2 The Golden Rule: Correlation Is Not Causation

This principle will protect you throughout your career.

Let's use a classic analogy. If you analyze data from a beach and discover that on days when ice cream sales increase, the number of shark attacks also increases. You can say they are correlated, meaning, the two numbers move in the same direction.

An inexperienced analyst might conclude: "Eating ice cream causes shark attacks!" A great analyst asks: "What else could be causing both of these things to happen?" The answer could be: a hot, sunny day.

More people go to the beach when it's sunny, which means more people are buying ice cream *and* more people are swimming in the ocean, which unfortunately leads to more encounters with sharks.

The temperature is the cause. Ice cream sales and shark attacks are separate outcomes influenced by the same underlying factor.

Always be skeptical. Whenever you see two variables moving together, stop and ask yourself: Is there a direct relationship, or is there a third factor influencing both?

Confusing correlation with causation can lead to costly and embarrassing conclusions. Let this principle guide your thinking.

> ⚠ *Warning: Common Pitfall*

> ***Correlation is Not Causation.*** *Never confuse the two in your analysis.*
>
> *Correlation means two things happen at the same time (e.g., ice cream sales and crime rates both go up in the summer).*
>
> *Causation means one thing directly causes the other (e.g., turning on a light switch causes the light to come on).*
>
> *As an analyst, your job is to find the* causal *link, not just the coincidence.*

2.3 A Quick Word on Bias

Finally, I want to introduce you to the idea of "bias" in data. Data does not always tell the full story. Sometimes the most important insight lies in what is missing. A classic example is survivorship bias.

During World War II, engineers wanted to add more armor to their bomber planes to protect them. They analyzed the planes that came *back* from missions and saw that they were covered in bullet holes on the wings, tail, and fuselage. The engine was almost always untouched.

The initial thought was: "Let's add more armor to the wings and tail, where all the bullet holes are!" But a clever statistician named Abraham Wald stopped them. He said, "No. Put the armor where there are *no* bullet holes on the engine."

His reasoning was simple but brilliant. The planes they were analyzing were the *survivors*. The reason they had no bullet holes on the engine was that the planes that *did* get hit in the engine never came back. The data they were looking at was biased because it was missing all the planes that didn't survive.

As an analyst, always ask: **"What data might I be missing? Whose story isn't being told by this dataset?"**

So, let's pause and take stock. You now have the three core pillars of the analyst's mindset:

- You know how to turn **vague problems into specific questions**.
- You understand the golden rule that **correlation is not causation.**
- You know how to ask, "What data am I missing?" to spot potential **bias**.

These mental tools are what separate a good analyst from a great one. They are your new lens for looking at the world.

But a mindset, as powerful as it is, needs a way to interact with the world. Just as a detective needs tools to investigate the crime scene, an analyst needs tools to investigate data. It's time to get your hands dirty and open up your very first and arguably most universal data toolkit.

In the next chapter, we are going to dive into a tool you may already be familiar with but have never used to its full potential: the spreadsheet. We will transform it from a simple list-maker into a powerful engine for analysis.

You will learn the formulas and techniques that professional analysts use every single day, and you will build your very first project for your portfolio. You've learned how to *think* like an analyst. Now, let's start *doing*.

Part 2

THE TECHNICAL TOOLKIT

Speaking the Language of Data

3

YOUR FIRST TOOLKIT

Mastering Spreadsheets

Welcome to your first real tool. In the last chapter, we forged your analyst's mindset. Now, it's time to pick up your first set of tools. We're starting with what might seem like a basic tool but is, in reality, one of the most powerful and universal pieces of software in the business world: **the spreadsheet.** Do not underestimate it.

3.1 Why I Took Spreadsheets Seriously (and You Should Too)

I didn't always respect Excel. Like many people, my first interaction with spreadsheets was simple record keeping during my internship as an accounting student in university. I knew how to enter numbers, maybe apply a bit of formatting. Excel felt ordinary. Replaceable.

That changed early in my data career. After completing my data training with Tech4Dev, months of theory and concepts, I joined a team where real analysis had to be done. One day, my manager asked me to analyze a dataset using Excel.

I opened the file confidently... and then reality hit. Rows everywhere. Multiple sheets. IDs that didn't match. Categories written three different ways. I spent **two full days** copying, pasting, manually checking values, and fixing errors I didn't even realize I was creating. I was exhausted, and still unsure my results were correct.

Then a senior analyst walked by. She glanced at my screen and said, "Why didn't you just use a VLOOKUP and a PivotTable?" In less than **two minutes,** she produced the exact analysis I had struggled with for two days. That was the moment I understood something important: **Excel wasn't basic. I was.**

What I saw as a grid of numbers was, in the right hands, a tool for speed, clarity, and leverage. That realization is why this chapter exists because if you don't master spreadsheets early, everything else in data will feel harder than it needs to be.

3.2 What Is a Spreadsheet and Why Should You Care?

A spreadsheet (like Microsoft Excel or Google Sheets) is basically a digital sheet that can do a lot more than writing. It's a grid made up of cells where you can:

- Store and organize data
- Clean messy information
- Perform logical calculations
- Summarize patterns
- Create simple visual reports

In many organizations, spreadsheets are the first place data lives before it ever reaches a database or advanced analytics tool. You might be thinking, "Isn't that for accountants?" While they certainly use it, here is the truth: **every professional, in every role, needs to know how to use a spreadsheet.**

From marketers tracking campaign results to project managers tracking timelines, spreadsheets are the common language of business data. For a data analyst, it is your foundational laboratory for exploring and understanding smaller datasets. Mastering it is non-negotiable. It is foundational.

3.3 The Core Concepts You MUST Know

Let's create a checklist of the core spreadsheet concepts. This is your learning guide. You can use this list to guide your future practice.

Spreadsheet Concepts Checklist:

- **Formulas & Functions:** The "brains" of the spreadsheet. These are commands that perform calculations (e.g., SUM, AVERAGE).

- **Sorting & Filtering:** The ability to rearrange your data or hide irrelevant information to focus on what matters.

- **Data Cleaning:** The process of fixing errors, removing duplicates, and standardizing data to make it reliable.

- **Conditional Formatting:** Automatically changing a cell's color based on its value (e.g., making all negative numbers red).

- **PivotTables:** A powerful feature that lets you summarize thousands of rows of data into a neat report in just a few clicks.

- **Basic Charting:** Creating visual representations of your data, like bar charts or line charts, to tell a story.

These six concepts are the bedrock of professional spreadsheet use. If you cannot confidently perform these tasks in a spreadsheet, pause your roadmap here and strengthen this foundation before moving forward.

3.4 Why This Stage Matters

Many aspiring analysts are eager to move quickly into programming languages and advanced tools. SQL sounds impressive. Python feels powerful. Machine learning appears exciting. As a result, spreadsheets are often treated as a temporary stop rather than a serious skill to develop.

This is a mistake.

Spreadsheets are where analytical discipline is formed. They force you to think about structure, consistency, and logic in a very direct way. When your formulas break, you see it immediately. When your categories are inconsistent, your summaries expose the error. When your data is messy, your results are unreliable. The feedback is instant, and that feedback trains you to be precise.

More importantly, spreadsheets teach you how to think in terms of rows, columns, conditions, and aggregations. These concepts are not limited to Excel or Google Sheets. They are foundational ideas that appear again in SQL, data visualization tools, and even in programming languages. When you eventually move to larger databases, you will realize that the environment has changed, but the logic remains the same.

Mastering spreadsheets at this stage reduces friction later. It builds confidence. It sharpens your analytical reasoning. It ensures that when you begin working with larger systems, you are not struggling with basic concepts while trying to learn advanced ones.

In this stage, you are not trying to become an Excel expert, but you are building structured thinking. And structured thinking is what defines a professional analyst.

3.5 Strengthening Your Skills

If you find that you are not yet comfortable cleaning datasets, applying logical rules, summarizing information, and presenting simple insights within a spreadsheet, it is important to slow down and strengthen this foundation before progressing further along the roadmap.

Learning in a rush often creates hidden gaps. Those gaps do not disappear. They resurface later, usually at the most inconvenient time, such as during a job interview or a work assignment. A strong foundation eliminates that risk.

To support your practical development, I have created structured guides that provide step by step walkthroughs for mastering spreadsheets at a deeper level. These resources expand on the concepts introduced in this chapter and are designed to help you build confidence through deliberate practice. You will find access details at the end of this book.

For now, focus on achieving comfort and clarity. You should be able to take a raw dataset, organize it logically, summarize its key patterns, and explain your findings clearly. When you can do that consistently, you are ready to move forward.

Spreadsheets are your first analytical environment. They are where you learn to control data rather than be overwhelmed by it. Once you are comfortable here, the transition to more advanced tools becomes significantly smoother.

In the next chapter, we will move from individual files to structured databases and begin learning the universal language used to query data at scale. It is time to take the next step.

3.6 Your Roadmap Checklist

Use this checklist to honestly assess your readiness before moving forward.

☐ I can take a messy dataset and clean it by removing duplicates, fixing inconsistent text, and standardizing categories.

☐ I understand how to apply logical rules to data, such as labeling, grouping, or categorizing records based on specific conditions.

☐ I can summarize large tables of data into meaningful totals, averages, or counts without manually calculating them.

☐ I am comfortable organizing data in a structured format so that it is easy to analyze and interpret.

☐ I can create a simple chart that communicates a clear insight rather than just displaying numbers.

☐ I can explain what I did in plain language, including how I cleaned the data and how I arrived at my conclusions.

If you cannot confidently check most of these boxes, pause here and strengthen your spreadsheet skills before progressing to the next stage of this roadmap.

A solid foundation will save you from confusion and frustration later.

Spreadsheets are not the final destination of your journey as a data analyst. They are your training ground. They teach structure, logic, and discipline. They allow you to understand how data behaves and how insights are extracted from it.

However, spreadsheets have limitations. They work well for small to medium datasets, but modern organizations often store millions of records in structured databases. At that scale, manual files are no longer efficient or sustainable. To work with data at that level, you need a new tool and a new language.

In the next chapter, we will move beyond individual files and begin learning SQL, the Structured Query Language used to communicate with databases. It is one of the most essential technical skills for any data analyst and a critical step forward on this roadmap.

4

SQL

The Lingua Franca of Data

Early in my career, I depended heavily on data engineers. Every analysis started with a request:

"Can you pull the customer list for me?"

"Can you help me add this column to the report?"

At first, it felt normal. After all, data engineers were experts in handling databases, right? But over time, the delays became frustrating. Simple requests took days. Follow-ups got stuck in queues. Deadlines approached while I waited. This wasn't because I couldn't analyze data, but it was because I couldn't access data independently.

One particular request changed everything. What should have been a quick pull dragged on for days. In that moment, I realized something uncomfortable: my biggest limitation wasn't my analytical thinking; it was my lack of SQL. That was when I decided to learn it.

Learning it wasn't easy. I spent hours staring at error messages, fixing commas, misspelling table names, and wondering why nothing worked. But eventually, something clicked. The first time I successfully joined two tables and retrieved exactly the dataset I needed, I experienced something new, **autonomy**.

That feeling of independence, speed, and control was different. SQL was the first tool that gave me true autonomy as a data analyst. And that's what this chapter is about: giving you that same freedom.

4.1 First, What Is a Database?

Before we learn the language, let's understand the environment it operates in. A database is simply a structured, organized collection of data, stored electronically. Unlike a single spreadsheet file, a database contains multiple related tables designed to work together.

There are many types of databases, but for now, you only need to know about two main categories:

- **Relational Databases (SQL Databases):** This is our entire focus as data analysts. In these databases, data is stored in tables with predefined columns and rows, just like a spreadsheet. The relational aspect is what makes these databases powerful. Tables can be linked to one another using a shared piece of information, such as an ID. This structure enables data to be connected across different parts of the system. For example, a Customers table can be linked to an Orders table using a CustomerID. This is the world where SQL lives. Examples include MySQL, PostgreSQL, and SQL Server.

- **Non-Relational Databases (NoSQL Databases):** You should know this term, but you don't need to learn it now. These databases are more flexible and don't always use the neat table structure. They are used for massive, unstructured data, like social media posts or complex web data. They use different query languages, not SQL. Examples include MongoDB and Cassandra.

Your takeaway: As a data analyst, you will spend 99% of your time working with **Relational (SQL) Databases**. That's why learning SQL is so critical.

In the last chapter, you proved you could analyze data and build a dashboard using a spreadsheet. You now have a solid foundation. But as we discussed, spreadsheets have a limit. What happens when your data has millions of rows, stored across multiple, complex tables in a company-wide system? You can't just open that in Excel. For that, you need to learn the language of databases: **SQL**.

4.2 What Is SQL and Why Is It So Important?

SQL (often pronounced "sequel") stands for **Structured Query Language**. It is the universal language used to communicate with and retrieve data from relational databases.

If a database is a massive, organized archive of information, SQL is the method you use to request exactly what you need. You do not open the entire system. You ask precise questions.

You specify:

- The columns you need
- The table(s) they come from
- The conditions that must be met
- How the results should be grouped or sorted

SQL allows you to extract, filter, summarize, and combine data at scale.

For a data analyst, knowing SQL is not optional. It is the single most in-demand, most critical technical skill you can possess. It is your key to unlocking the vast stores of data that companies collect every day.

4.3 The Core Concepts You MUST Know

A database is a collection of related tables. A table is just a grid of rows and columns, like a spreadsheet. The power comes from using SQL to select, filter, and combine these tables.

You do not need to memorize every command immediately. But you must understand these foundational commands:

SQL Concepts Checklist:

- **SELECT & FROM:** The most basic query. SELECT specifies the columns you want, and FROM specifies the table you want them from.

- **WHERE:** The filter. This lets you add conditions to your query to retrieve only the data you need.

- **ORDER BY:** The sorter. This allows you to sort your results in ascending or descending order.

- **GROUP BY & COUNT/SUM/AVG:** The summarizer. GROUP BY is the SQL equivalent of a PivotTable, allowing you to aggregate data. COUNT, SUM, and AVG are aggregate functions you use with it.

- **JOIN:** The connector. It allows you to combine rows from two or more tables based on a related column between them.

These concepts form the backbone of SQL. Mastery of them allows you to answer real business questions using structured data.

4.4 Why SQL Changes Everything

Spreadsheets are powerful, but they are limited by size and structure. Organizations, however, store data across millions of records in centralized systems. SQL allows you to operate confidently in that environment.

More importantly, it changes your professional positioning. When you can query databases independently, you move from being someone who waits for data to someone who drives analysis proactively. You become faster. More reliable. More valuable. That shift matters.

4.5 Strengthening Your SQL Skills

If you are not yet comfortable writing queries that retrieve, filter, summarize, and combine data, it is worth investing time to strengthen this area before progressing further. Like spreadsheets, SQL builds logical discipline. The difference is scale.

To support your development, I have created structured guides that provide step by step walkthroughs for mastering SQL in a practical and business focused way. You will find access details at the end of this book.

For now, focus on understanding how databases are structured and how SQL allows you to ask precise questions within that structure. Once you can confidently retrieve and combine data from multiple tables, you are ready for the next stage of the roadmap.

4.6 Your Roadmap Checklist

☐ I understand how relational databases organize data into related tables.

☐ I can retrieve specific columns from a table using SQL.

☐ I can filter results based on defined conditions.

☐ I can summarize data using aggregate functions.

☐ I understand how related tables can be combined logically.

If you cannot confidently check most of these boxes, pause here and deepen your SQL foundation before moving forward.

You can now extract and analyze data from professional-grade databases. You don't have to depend on data engineers for every project. But how do you communicate your findings? Confusing charts can mislead stakeholders, and SQL cannot turn complex data into clear insights.

In the next chapter, we will learn how to use Power BI and Tableau for data visualization. With this, you will tell impactful stories with data and drive action by helping stakeholders make informed decisions.

5

DATA VISUALIZATION

From Numbers to Narratives

You have come a long way. You can organize data in spreadsheets. You can retrieve it from databases using SQL. You now have access to structured information. But access is not the same as influence.

An analysis that lives in a table is incomplete. Your responsibility as a data analyst is not only to discover insights but to communicate them clearly and convincingly. This is where data visualization becomes essential.

5.1 Why Visualization Matters More Than You Think

I still remember building my first dashboard in Tableau. It had everything, or so I thought. Multiple charts on a single tab. Different colors everywhere. Filters, numbers, trends. I was proud of the work I had done.

What I didn't realize was that I had built a collection of visuals, and not a story. After presenting the results of my analysis to my boss, I expected quick approval. Instead, he looked at the dashboard, paused, and said, "I don't get it. Refine this and make it better."

We went back and forth more than once. The analysis itself was correct. The numbers were solid. But the message wasn't landing.

I went back to the dashboard and approached it differently. I reduced the number of charts. Fixed the inconsistent colors. Reordered the visuals. Most importantly, I thought about the story, the question I was answering, and the decision the viewer needed to make.

An hour later, I presented a new version. This time, there were no questions. Just clarity. That experience taught me something fundamental. **The best analysis is useless if people can't understand it.**

A well-designed chart answers a question before it is asked. A poorly designed one creates more confusion. Your goal is not to impress with complexity. It is to communicate with clarity.

In this chapter, you'll learn how to present your analysis, so the message is obvious and the insight is impossible to miss.

5.2 Principles of Effective Visualization

Before we even open a tool, we need to internalize the principles that separate a confusing chart from a clear one. These are not steps to follow, but rules to guide your thinking. A great analyst *always* keeps this in mind.

Principle 1: Choose the Right Chart for the Job

This is the most important decision you'll make. Your goal is to match your chart to your message.

- To compare values between categories, **use a Bar Chart.**
- To show a trend over a period of time, **use a Line Chart.**
- To show the relationship between two numbers, **use a Scatter Plot.**
- To display geographical data, **use a Map.**

Principle 2: Use Color with Purpose

Color should be used to highlight key information or to distinguish categories, not to decorate. Keep your color palette simple and accessible to avoid creating a "rainbow effect" that confuses the viewer.

Principle 3: Eliminate Clutter

Every element on your chart should serve a purpose. Be ruthless in removing unnecessary background lines, borders, and distracting labels. The data itself should always be the hero of the story.

Principle 4: Label Clearly and Concisely

Your chart should be understandable in seconds without needing a manual. Ensure it has a clear title that describes the main insight, labeled axes, and a legend only if necessary.

These principles transform visuals from decorative graphics into decision-making tools.

5.3 The Role of BI Tools

So, how do we apply these principles? To apply these principles on a scale, analysts use Business Intelligence tools such as Power BI or Tableau. These tools are undisputed leaders in the industry.

They allow you to:

- Connect to structured data sources
- Create interactive dashboards
- Apply filters dynamically
- Build calculated metrics
- Share insights with stakeholders

You don't need to learn both right now. They are very similar, and skills in one tool are easily transferable to the other. I recommend starting with **Power BI** if you are familiar with the Microsoft ecosystem (Excel, etc.), or **Tableau** if you want to focus on a tool famous for its beautiful and highly flexible visualizations. Both have excellent free versions (Power BI Desktop and Tableau Public) that are perfect for learning.

Remember: the tool does not make the analyst effective. The thinking does.

5.4 Your Power BI / Tableau Learning Roadmap

This checklist is your roadmap to the essential features you need to learn as a beginner in either tool.

BI Tool Learning Checklist

- **Connecting to Data:** Learn how to import data from different sources (especially CSV files and Excel).

- **Understanding the Interface:** Identify the main components: the data pane (your fields), the visualizations pane (your chart types), and the canvas (your workspace).

- **Dimensions vs. Measures:** Master the difference between your descriptive categories (**Dimensions**) and the numbers you want to analyze (**Measures**). This is fundamental.

- **Building Basic Charts:** Practice creating the core four: bar charts, line charts, maps, and scatter plots by dragging and dropping fields.

- **Calculated Fields (or DAX Basics in Power BI):** Learn to create a simple calculated field to derive new data (e.g., Profit = Sales - Cost).

- **Filtering Data:** Understand how to apply filters to a single chart and to an entire dashboard page.

- **Dashboard Assembly & Interactivity:** Learn how to combine multiple charts onto a single dashboard and, crucially, how to make them interact with each other (e.g., clicking a country on a map filters a bar chart).

5.5 Why This Skill Elevates You

Many analysts can retrieve data. Fewer can present it in a way that drives action. Visualization bridges the gap between technical work and executive decision-making. It translates complexity into clarity. It ensures that your insights are not only correct but understood.

When you can combine structured analysis with clear communication, you become significantly more valuable within any organization. You are no longer just someone who works with data. You are someone who influences decisions.

5.6 Your Roadmap Checklist

☐ I can choose appropriate chart types based on the question being answered.

☐ I can design a dashboard that prioritizes clarity over decoration.

☐ I understand how to structure visuals so that they tell a coherent story.

☐ I can explain the key insight of a chart in one or two sentences.

If you cannot confidently check most of these boxes, take time to strengthen your visualization skills before moving on.

You now understand how to retrieve and communicate data effectively. For many readers, this marks the completion of the essential technical foundation of a data analyst.

However, if you are eager to deepen your technical toolkit even further, there is one more powerful tool to explore. In the next chapter, we will introduce you to the world of programming with **Python**.

6

PYTHON

Your Analytical Power Tool

Welcome to the final chapter of our technical journey. Before we begin, I want you to pause for a moment and take a deep breath. You have already built the complete, job-ready skillset of a highly effective data analyst. With spreadsheets, SQL, and a BI tool, you are more than prepared to land your first role.

This chapter is an optional power-up. It's for those of you who are feeling confident and are curious about what lies beyond the core toolkit. It's a glimpse into the world of programming, designed to show you how it can make you an even more powerful analyst in the long run.

6.1 What Is Python, and Why Should I Care?

At its core, Python is a programming language. It is a language that lets you give step-by-step instructions to your computer.

Using tools like Excel or Power BI is like choosing options from a menu that's already been created. But with Python, you're writing the steps yourself which gives you more control, more flexibility, and the freedom to decide exactly how things should work.

You would use Python when you need to do something that your BI tool or spreadsheet software can't do easily. For example:

- **To automate a boring, repetitive task:** Imagine you have to download and clean the same report every single Monday morning. With Python, you can write a script to do this for you automatically
- **To perform very complex cleaning:** What if you have a column of text that needs 10 different cleaning steps applied in a specific order? This is tedious in Excel but simple in Python.
- **To work with truly massive files:** When you have a file with five million rows that would instantly crash Excel, Python can handle it without breaking a sweat.

In other words, Python expands what is possible.

6.2 Where Python Fits in Your Growth

At this stage of your journey, it is important to understand that Python is not a requirement for entry into the field. Many analysts build successful early careers using spreadsheets, SQL, and visualization tools alone. These tools cover the majority of business reporting and operational analytics needs. However, Python becomes valuable when the complexity of your work increases.

As datasets grow larger, workflows become repetitive, business questions become more sophisticated, and manual processes begin to feel limiting. You may find yourself exporting data repeatedly, applying the same cleaning steps week after week, or struggling to manipulate large files efficiently. This is often the moment when Python transitions from "optional" to "strategic."

Python fits into your growth as a multiplier. It does not replace your foundational skills; it extends them. The filtering logic you learned in SQL, the aggregation principles you practiced in spreadsheets, and the storytelling discipline you developed in visualization tools all transfer directly into Python-based analysis.

The difference lies in control and scalability. With Python, you are not constrained by menus or predefined buttons. You can define your own workflows, automate your own processes, and handle volumes of data that exceed the limits of traditional tools.

For some analysts, Python becomes a gateway into advanced analytics, including predictive modeling and machine learning. For others, it remains a powerful automation tool that increases efficiency and reliability. Both paths are valid. The key is understanding that Python is part of your evolution, not your starting point.

6.3 What You Actually Use Python For as a Data Analyst

When people first approach Python, they often get stuck in abstract programming exercises that feel disconnected from real work. While understanding basic concepts such as variables and data types is important, your focus as a data analyst should remain hands-on.

You are not learning Python to build mobile apps. You are learning Python to work with data more efficiently.

In real analytical environments, Python is typically used for the following tasks:

Load and explore structured datasets: You should be able to import a dataset into your environment and quickly inspect its structure. This includes understanding how many rows and columns it has, identifying data types, and spotting obvious inconsistencies.

Clean and prepare data systematically: Much of analytical work involves preparing data before analysis. This may include renaming columns, standardizing text values, handling missing entries, converting data types, or removing duplicates. Python allows these transformations to be performed systematically and reproducibly.

Filter and subset data: Just as you would filter rows in SQL or apply conditions in Excel, you should be able to isolate specific subsets of data based on defined criteria.

Create derived metrics: In many analyses, you need derived metrics. For example, calculating profit from revenue and cost, or computing growth rates between periods. Python enables you to create new columns based on logical expressions.

Aggregate and summarize: Grouping data to compute totals, averages, or counts is fundamental to analysis. The same thinking you applied with PivotTables or GROUP BY statements carries over directly into Python.

Export results for reporting: After cleaning and transforming data, you should be able to export the refined dataset for visualization, reporting, or further modeling.

These are the everyday uses of Python in analytics. Notice that none of them require advanced computer science knowledge. They require structured thinking and comfort with data.

6.4 The Role of Pandas

For beginner and intermediate analysts, the most important Python library is Pandas. It provides a structured, table-like environment where you can manipulate data in a way that mirrors spreadsheet logic but with greater scalability.

When using Pandas, your goal is not to memorize syntax but to understand how to manipulate structured datasets programmatically.

At a minimum, you should be comfortable with:

- **Understanding the Environment:** Learn how to open a notebook, write text, and run a code cell.

- **Importing the Library:** The first step in any script: import pandas as pd.

- **DataFrames & Series:** Understanding that a **DataFrame** is the whole table, and a **Series** is a single column.

- **Reading Data:** Using the pd.read_csv() function to load a spreadsheet into a DataFrame.

- **Inspecting Your Data:** Using .head() to see the first few rows and .info() to get a summary of your data's structure.

- **Selecting & Filtering:** Grabbing a specific column (df['column_name']) or filtering for rows that meet a condition (df[df['Sales'] > 1000]).

- **Handling Missing Values:** Finding missing data with .isnull() and deciding whether to drop it (.dropna()) or fill it (.fillna()).

If you can perform these tasks, you are already using Python in a way that meaningfully enhances your analytical workflow.

There is no need to rush into advanced libraries or complex modeling techniques. Mastery of structured data manipulation alone can significantly increase your efficiency and professional value.

6.5 Your Roadmap Checklist

Use this checklist to assess your readiness and mindset.

☐ I understand that Python is an enhancement tool, not a requirement for entry level analyst roles.

☐ I can identify scenarios where automation would improve my workflow.

☐ I am comfortable manipulating structured datasets programmatically.

☐ I recognize that analytical thinking matters more for a data analyst than writing complex code.

☐ I feel no pressure to rush this stage of the roadmap.

If you cannot confidently check most of these boxes, revisit the strategic intent of this chapter before moving forward.

You have now explored the full technical landscape of modern data analysis. Spreadsheets built your structure. SQL gave you access to data at scale. Visualization strengthened your communication. Python introduced automation and extensibility.

The hard skills are in place. Now, it's time for the final, most important part of our journey: turning those skills into a career.

In Part 3, we will shift our focus entirely to building your professional presence. We'll craft your portfolio, write your resume, and prepare you to confidently walk into interviews and land your first data analyst job. Let's go get your job.

Part 3

YOUR CAREER LAUNCH KIT

7

BUILDING YOUR PROFESSIONAL PORTFOLIO

Welcome to Part 3, your career launch kit. Up until now, we've been focused on building your skills. Now, we shift our focus to one of the most critical parts of your job search: **proving your skills to employers.** In data analytics, skills alone are not enough. Employers need evidence, and your portfolio is that evidence.

Let me be direct: in the world of data analytics, your portfolio is more important than your resume. A resume *tells* people what you can do. A portfolio *shows* them. It is your single greatest asset.

7.1 What Is a Portfolio and Why Does It Matter?

A portfolio is simply a collection of your best projects, organized in one place online. It's a gallery where you showcase your work.

When a hiring manager is looking at two candidates with similar resumes, the one with a clean, well-explained portfolio immediately stands out.

Your portfolio proves three critical things:

- You possess practical technical skills. (Excel, SQL, Power BI).
- You have the **initiative** to learn and build things on your own.
- You can **communicate** your analytical process and findings clearly.

That last point is essential. Employers are not hiring applicants who can merely write queries. They are hiring smart analysts who can solve problems and explain the solution.

Each project in your portfolio should answer four simple questions:

- What problem were you solving?
- What steps did you take?
- What tools did you use?
- What insight did you discover?

If someone can understand those four things quickly, your portfolio is doing its job.

7.2 Your Portfolio Structure: Technical Depth and Visual Clarity

An effective portfolio has two complementary components:

- **The Technical Repository:** This is where your detailed work lives. It includes your SQL queries, spreadsheets, dashboards, notebooks, and documentation. It shows depth and authenticity.
- **The Presentation Layer:** This is the clean, accessible front door to your work. It makes your projects easy to evaluate.

Together, these two layers balance credibility and clarity.

7.3 Building a Strong Technical Repository

The industry standard for hosting technical projects is GitHub. If you have never used GitHub before, do not worry. At a beginner level, it is simply a professional online folder for your projects.

You do not need advanced coding knowledge to use GitHub effectively. You only need to understand three simple concepts:

Your Profile

This is your personal page. It includes your name, a short bio, and your pinned projects.

A Repository

A repository is simply a folder for one project. Each project should have its own repository.

A README File

This is the most important file in your repository. It explains your project in clear business language.

7.4 How to Structure Each Project

The strength of your portfolio does not come from complexity. It comes from clarity. Inside each project folder on GitHub (which is called a "repository"), you will create a single text file called a **README.md**.

This is the most important part of your GitHub. It's the description that explains your project to a hiring manager. A good README answers four key questions.

Here is a simple, effective template. Copy and paste this into a text file named README.md for each of your projects.

Project: [Name of Your Project]

The Problem / Business Question:

(In one or two sentences, describe the goal of the project. What question were you trying to answer?)

Example: "The goal of this project was to analyze a year's worth of credit card transactions to understand my personal spending habits and identify opportunities for savings."

The Process / What I Did:

(In a few bullet points, describe the steps you took. Be specific.)

Example:

- *Cleaned and standardized the raw data in Excel, fixing inconsistent category names and removing duplicate entries.*
- *Used a PivotTable to summarize total spending by category and by month.*

- *Created a bar chart to visualize the top 5 spending categories and a line chart to track spending over time.*

The Tools I Used:

(Simply list the tools you used for the project.)

Example: Microsoft Excel, PivotTables, SUMIFS

The Insight / My Findings:

(In one or two sentences, what was the main takeaway from your analysis? What did you learn?)

Example: "My analysis revealed that over 40% of my monthly spending was on 'Dining Out' and 'Subscriptions,' highlighting a clear area to focus on for budget cuts."

(Optional but highly recommended: Add a screenshot of your finished dashboard or chart here!)

7.5 Do You Need a Portfolio Website?

Once your projects are organized on GitHub, you may choose to create a simple portfolio website. This is not mandatory at the beginning.

A website simply makes it easier for recruiters to view your work in one place. It can include:

- A short professional summary
- Links to your top projects
- Contact information

There are many tools available to build a simple website, including GitHub Pages or website builders. The specific tool is less important than clarity and professionalism. If building a website feels overwhelming right now, start with GitHub. Improve it. Then expand later.

7.6 How Many Projects Do You Need?

Three strong projects are enough to begin applying for roles. Each project should demonstrate a different skill:

- One spreadsheet or data cleaning project
- One SQL-based project
- One visualization dashboard project

Quality matters more than quantity.

Avoid copying tutorials without adding your own interpretation. Even if you use a public dataset, add your own framing and insights.

Original thought is what separates you from everyone else learning online.

7.7 Your Roadmap Checklist

☐ I have at least three well-documented projects.

☐ Each project clearly explains the problem, process, tools, and insight.

☐ My GitHub profile is clean and professional.

☐ A hiring manager can understand my work within five minutes.

If you cannot confidently check most of these boxes, refine your portfolio before applying for jobs.

You now have more than skills. You have proof. But what if you want to stand out even further? What if you want to tailor your portfolio toward a specific industry such as finance, healthcare, or marketing?

In the next chapter, we will explore how to design a distinctive project that positions you strategically in the job market.

8

YOUR NEXT PROJECT

Strategic Map of Ideas

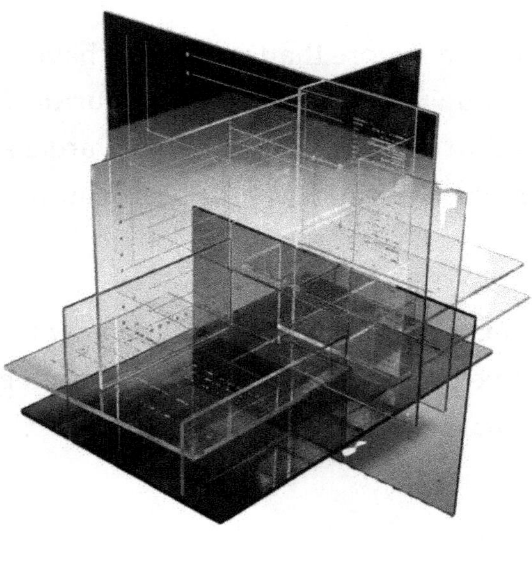

By now, you understand the core toolkit of a data analyst. You know how to think analytically. You can work with spreadsheets, retrieve data using SQL, design clear visualizations, and even extend your workflow with Python if needed.

At this stage, you should be building or refining projects for your portfolio. For many beginners, three solid projects demonstrating different skills are enough to begin applying for roles. But if you want to stand out, truly stand out, there is one more powerful move you can make.

Create a project that is **uniquely yours**. A project driven by your own curiosity. This chapter will guide you in identifying the right data and shaping the right idea for that project.

8.1 Why a Personal Project Matters

Hiring managers review dozens, sometimes hundreds, of portfolios. Many candidates showcase similar guided exercises or commonly replicated datasets. A personal project changes the narrative.

It communicates that you are not just consuming content. You are creating insight. A unique, personal project instantly signals three things:

Passion

It shows you are genuinely interested in the field, not just following a tutorial.

Initiative

It proves you can manage a project from start to finish on your own.

Problem-Solving Skills

It demonstrates your ability to formulate your own questions and seek out answers from the data.

In interviews, a personal project gives you something unique to talk about. Instead of repeating what hundreds of other candidates have done, you can explain your own reasoning, challenges, and discoveries. That authenticity is powerful.

In real business environments, problems are rarely handed to you with step-by-step instructions. The ability to frame a question and explore it thoughtfully is what separates a developing analyst from a job-ready one.

8.2 Choosing a Project Intentionally

Choosing a dataset randomly is easy. Choosing strategically requires thought. Before downloading anything, ask yourself three questions:

- What industries interest me long term?
- What type of role do I see myself in?
- What problems do I naturally find interesting?

Your answers should guide your choice.

- If you are drawn to finance, exploring transaction data or investment trends makes sense.
- If you are interested in healthcare, analyzing public health indicators strengthens your positioning.
- If marketing excites you, studying consumer behavior or campaign performance aligns with your goals.

The closer your project aligns with your intended career path, the stronger your professional narrative becomes. When employers see alignment between your portfolio and their industry, it reduces perceived risk. You appear intentional rather than exploratory.

8.3 Where to Find High-Quality Data

One of the most common questions I receive is, "Where do I find data?" You would be surprised how much high-quality, free data is available online. Here are reliable starting points:

- **Kaggle Datasets:** This is the most popular and arguably the best place to start. It has thousands of datasets on every topic imaginable, from "Netflix Movies and TV Shows" to "Heart Attack Analysis & Prediction." It's a playground for data analysts.

- **Google Dataset Search:** It is a search engine specifically for datasets. It's a powerful tool for finding data on more obscure or specific topics.

- **Data.gov:** The home of the U.S. Government's open data. You can find incredible datasets here on everything from public health statistics to airline on-time performance. Many other countries have similar portals (e.g., data.gov.uk).

- **FiveThirtyEight:** This renowned data journalism website shares the data behind many of their fascinating articles on politics, sports, and culture. Their datasets are always clean and interesting.

- **Awesome Public Datasets on GitHub:** This is a massive, curated list of high-quality datasets, organized by topic. It's a fantastic resource for browsing and getting inspired.

When selecting a dataset, evaluate:

- Is the data sufficiently detailed to answer meaningful questions?
- Is it manageable given my current skill level?
- Does it align with my professional direction?

Choose thoughtfully. Depth of analysis matters more than dataset size.

8.4 What Should Your Project Be About?

The best project is one you are genuinely curious about. Follow your passion. Here are some ideas, categorized by interest, to get you started.

If you love Movies & TV:

- Analyze the IMDb Top 250 movies. What's the average runtime? Which directors appear most often?

- Explore the Netflix dataset on Kaggle. Are there trends in the types of content added over the years?

If you love Sports:

- Analyze F1 racing data. How does starting position correlate with final race position at different tracks?
- Explore NBA player stats. What are the statistical characteristics of an MVP-winning season?

If you love Business & Finance:

- Analyze a dataset of Zillow housing prices. What are the most expensive zip codes in a given state?
- Explore a dataset of startup funding. Do startups in certain industries receive more funding on average?

If you love Health & Fitness:

- Analyze your own fitness tracker data (most apps let you export it). What's the relationship between your daily steps and your sleep quality?

- Explore public health data on smoking or obesity rates. Are there correlations with income or education levels?

The topic matters less than your clarity of question and quality of explanation. Always begin with a focused question.

- Not "explore this dataset."
- But "What factors are associated with higher performance?"
  Or "How has this trend changed over time?"
  Or "What patterns emerge across regions?"

Clear questions lead to clear analysis.

8.5 Common Mistakes to Avoid

As you design your personal project, be mindful of these pitfalls:

- Choosing a dataset that is too advanced for your current level, leading to frustration and incomplete work.

- Focusing on flashy techniques instead of clarity and explanation.

- Skipping documentation or failing to explain your reasoning.
- Overcomplicating visuals instead of highlighting insight.

Remember: your goal is not to impress with complexity. Your goal is to demonstrate structured thinking and sound judgment.

8.6 Your Roadmap Checklist

☐ I have identified an industry or topic that genuinely interests me.

☐ I have selected a dataset aligned with that interest.

☐ I have defined at least one clear analytical question.

☐ I understand how this project strengthens my professional positioning.

When you add a personal, strategically aligned project to your portfolio, your profile becomes more than competent. It becomes intentional.

You have the skills, you have the proof, and you have a story to tell. Now, it's time to craft that story. In the next chapter, we will take all your hard work, skills and projects, and learn how to present it professionally on your resume and cover letter. Let's get you ready for the job market.

9

CRAFTING YOUR RESUME & COVER LETTER

You have the skills. You have the portfolio. Now, we need to build the bridge that connects your abilities to a hiring manager's attention. That bridge is your resume.

Let's be clear about the goal: **the purpose of your resume is not to get you a job. It's to get you an interview.** It's a 15-second advertisement for your skills. It needs to be clean, impactful, and tailored. In this chapter, we will build that advertisement.

9.1 The Anatomy of a Perfect Data Analyst Resume

Forget complicated layouts, multiple columns, graphics, and creative fonts. Your resume must be readable by both a human recruiter and the software they use to scan applications. That software is called an Applicant Tracking System, or ATS.

To maximize clarity and compatibility, use a clean, single column format. Your resume should include the following key sections:

Contact Information

Your Name, Phone Number, Email, and, most importantly, a clickable link to your new Portfolio Website.

Your portfolio is your proof. Make it easy to find.

Summary

This is a short two-to-three-line positioning statement at the top of your resume. It should reflect who you are professionally and what value you offer.

Example: "Aspiring Data Analyst with a strong foundation in SQL, Power BI, and Excel. Passionate about translating complex data into actionable business insights and clear visualizations."

Keep it focused. Avoid vague phrases like "hardworking" or "team player." Anchor your summary in skills and value.

Technical Skills

A simple, clean, categorized list of your technical skills. Examples:

- **Languages:** SQL, Python (Basic)
- **BI & Visualizations:** Power BI, Tableau, Excel (PivotTables, XLOOKUP)

- **Databases:** PostgreSQL, MySQL

Keep it honest. Only list tools that you can confidently discuss in an interview.

Projects

This is the most important section of your resume. Here, you will list the projects from your portfolio. If you do not have years of professional experience, your projects demonstrate your readiness.

Each project should include:

- Project title
- One line summary of the business question
- Two to three impact focused bullet points

We will refine those bullet points in the next section.

Experience

Even if your previous job was not in analytics, you can frame it strategically. Think in terms of data and results.

Instead of writing:

Handled customer complaints

Write:

Analyzed recurring customer complaints to identify patterns, contributing to a process improvement that reduced response time.

Employers care about problem solving, ownership, and measurable thinking.

Education

List your degree, institution, and graduation year. If you have relevant certifications, include them here.

9.2 The Impact Formula for Bullet Points

"Responsible for analyzing data" is a terrible bullet point. It's passive and tells the recruiter nothing. We are going to use a simple, powerful formula to write bullet points that show *impact*.

The Formula: Performed Action to achieve Result using Tool.

Let's apply this to the projects you've already completed:

- **Before:** Used SQL for a music store project

- **After:** Analyzed a relational music store database to identify top revenue generating customers using SQL, JOIN and GROUP BY queries.

- **Before:** Made a dashboard for global trends
- **After:** Developed an interactive Power BI dashboard to visualize global development indicators, enabling users to filter by country and year for targeted insights.

- **Before:** Personal budget project in Excel
- **After:** Cleaned and analyzed one year of transaction data in Excel to identify key spending categories and highlight potential cost reduction opportunities.

Did you notice the improvements? The "After" versions are specific, results-oriented, and packed with keywords.

9.3 Writing a Cover Letter That Actually Works

Do you need a cover letter? Yes, but not the kind you think. A cover letter is not a long, boring summary of your resume. It's a short, sharp note that answers one question for the recruiter: **"Why should I care about *this* applicant for *this* specific job?"**

Here is a simple 3-paragraph template that works every time.

Paragraph 1: The Hook

State the exact role you're applying for and express genuine enthusiasm for the company. Mention one specific thing you admire about their work, their product, or their mission.

Paragraph 2: The Connection

This is the most important part. Pick two or three key requirements from the job description and directly connect them to your projects or skills.

- *Example: "I saw that you require strong experience with Power BI. In my 'Global Trends' portfolio project, I built a fully interactive dashboard that handled over 50,000 rows of data. I am confident I can bring this skill to your team to help you visualize your marketing data more effectively."*

Paragraph 3: The Close

Reiterate your interest and state your confidence in your ability to contribute. End with a clear call to action. "I am eager to discuss how my analytical skills can benefit your team and have attached my resume for your review."

That's it. Short, targeted, and respectful of the recruiter's time.

9.4 Cover Letter Sample

Theory is good, but seeing a real example is better. Let's imagine you are applying for a "Junior Data Analyst" role at a fictional company called "Innovate Inc." The job description mentions they are looking for someone with "experience in Power BI" and "strong SQL skills."

Here is a complete cover letter you could write, using our 3-paragraph template and referencing the projects from your portfolio.

Dear Hiring Team,

I am writing to express my interest in the Junior Data Analyst position at Innovate Inc. I am particularly impressed by your commitment to improving customer experience through data driven decision making.

Your job description emphasizes strong skills in SQL and Power BI. In my portfolio projects, I have applied both tools in practical settings. I used SQL to analyze relational datasets and identify key revenue drivers, and I developed interactive Power BI dashboards that transformed raw data into clear, actionable insights. These experiences have strengthened my ability to translate business questions into structured analysis.

My resume, which is attached for your review, provides further detail on my skills and project work. I am incredibly eager for the opportunity to discuss how my passion for data storytelling and my technical abilities can contribute to the success of Innovate Inc. Thank you for your time and consideration.

Sincerely,
[Your Name]

You now have the two key documents you need for your job search. You have a story, and you know how to tell it.

9.5 Final Advice Before You Apply

Before sending any application, ask yourself:

- Is my resume tailored to this specific role?
- Have I used clear, impact driven bullet points?
- Does my cover letter directly connect my experience to your needs?

Small adjustments can significantly increase your response rate from recruiters. Applying blindly with the same resume to every role is rarely effective. Intentional applications outperform volume.

9.6 Your Roadmap Checklist

☐ I have created a clean, single column resume.

☐ My bullet points follow the impact formula.

☐ My portfolio link is clearly visible.

☐ I have written a short, targeted cover letter template.

☐ I tailor my resume slightly for each application.

You now have your skills, proof, and positioning. But sending applications into the void is the slowest way to land a role.

In the next chapter, we will discuss a faster strategy: building relationships, networking strategically, and navigating interviews with confidence. It is time to move from preparation to opportunity.

10

NAVIGATING THE JOB MARKET

Networking & Interviews

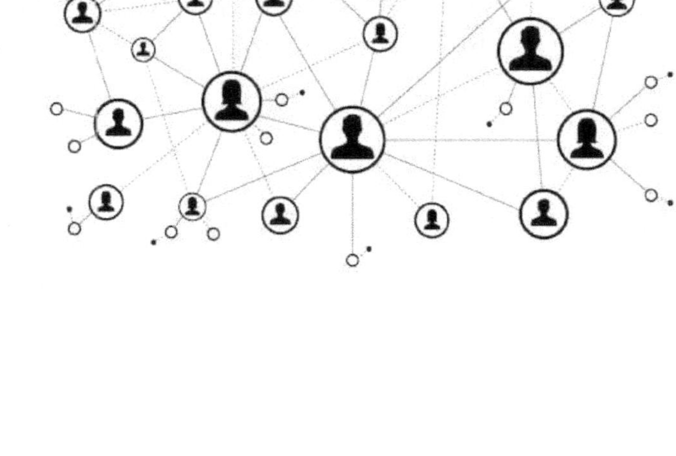

You have your resume in hand and your portfolio is live. You are ready, but a successful job search is not built on repeatedly clicking "Apply" and hoping something sticks. That approach relies too heavily on luck.

A strategic job search puts you in a position where luck is no longer the main factor. In this chapter, we'll focus on the two pillars that move the needle: **networking (done the right way)** and **interviewing (done with intention).**

10.1 Your Professional storefront: Mastering LinkedIn

Before you send a single application, you need to get LinkedIn right. Recruiters live on LinkedIn. Hiring managers check LinkedIn. Referrals start on LinkedIn. Long before you submit an application, they are already searching, observing, and forming impressions.

Whether you like it or not, **your LinkedIn profile is your professional storefront**. Let's make sure it's open for business.

"Recruiter-Ready" LinkedIn Checklist:

A Professional Headshot: A clear, friendly photo of your face. No logos, no pets, no group photos.

An Optimized Headline: This is the most important real estate on your profile. Don't just put "Student." Be aspirational and keyword-focused.

- *Good:* "Aspiring Data Analyst"
- *Better:* "Aspiring Data Analyst | SQL | Power BI | Excel"
- *Best:* "Data Analyst specializing in Business Intelligence and Data Visualization"

A Compelling "About" Section: This is a slightly longer version of your resume summary.

In 3–4 sentences, state the following:

- Who you are
- The tools you use (SQL, Power BI, Excel, Python)
- The kinds of problems you enjoy solving

A Featured Section
This is critical. Add:

- Your portfolio website

- Links to your best projects. If this section is empty, you're leaving opportunities on the table.

A Strong Skills Section
Add all relevant skills you've learned and ask a few colleagues or friends to endorse your top three. It helps with search visibility.

10.2 Networking by Creating Value

Networking often feels uncomfortable because people associate it with asking for something. Let's redefine it. Networking is building professional relationships through shared interest and contribution. You do not begin by asking. You begin by contributing.

When I first started my career, I was overwhelmed by the sheer volume of conflicting advice. I saw so many talented people struggle to find their footing, not because they lacked intelligence, but because they lacked a clear map.

My LinkedIn journey didn't begin with a job search. It began with a simple desire to help. I started sharing short, straightforward explanations of things I had just learned, posts like *"What is a PivotTable?"* or *"The easiest way to understand an INNER JOIN."*

I wasn't trying to sound like a senior expert. I was simply positioning myself as someone who could explain things clearly, in a way beginners could actually understand and as a **trusted guide** who was actively simplifying the journey for others.

The challenge I faced was not technical; it was finding the courage to share. I worried my posts were too simple or that I wasn't experienced enough. But I shared it anyway.

The thing is, I'm forever grateful I did, because people started following me, asking questions, and thanking me for the clarity. My profile quickly became a resource hub for data newbies. That consistency did two powerful things.

First, it deepened my own understanding. Teaching forced me to think clearly and truly master the fundamentals.

Second, it shaped my professional identity. Recruiters and hiring managers didn't just see someone who worked with data, they saw someone who could communicate it. Someone who could simplify complexity. Someone who could lead.

That's when I realized this: your LinkedIn profile is not just a place to list your skills. It's a place to demonstrate how you think, explain, and add value.

Even as a beginner, you can:

- Share what you are learning
- Reflect on a project you completed
- Explain a concept in your own words
- Comment thoughtfully on industry posts

In this chapter, I'll show you how to move beyond passive job applications and use intentional networking to build relationships that open real doors.

10.3 Networking for People Who Dislike Networking

The word "networking" can sound scary. It brings up images of awkward conversations and asking for favors. Let's redefine it. For us, networking is simply **making human connections based on shared professional interests.**

Here's how to do it in a low-stress, genuine way:

Engage, Don't Just Connect

Follow data analytics leaders and companies you admire on LinkedIn. Don't just be a silent observer. When someone posts an interesting article or dashboard, leave a thoughtful comment. Ask a question. Share your perspective. This is how you get on people's radar naturally.

The Informational Interview

This is the most powerful networking tool. You are not asking for a job. You are asking for 15 minutes of someone's time to hear about their experience. People generally love to talk about their work.

Here is a simple, respectful template to send as a connection request or a short message on LinkedIn:

"Hi [Name], my name is [Your Name] and I'm an aspiring data analyst. I came across your profile and was really impressed by your work at [Their Company]. If you have 15 minutes to spare in the coming weeks, I'd be grateful for the chance to hear a bit about your journey in the field. I'm just starting out and would truly value your perspective."

Most people won't respond, and that's okay. But the few who do will provide you with invaluable advice and a genuine connection in the industry.

10.4 Acing the Interview Gauntlet

An interview for a data analyst role is usually a multi-stage process. Let's break down the typical "gauntlet" so you know exactly what to expect.

Stage 1: The HR / Recruiter Screen

Goal: To see if you are a normal, pleasant person with good communication skills who meets the basic qualifications.

Common Questions:

- "Tell me about yourself." (Have a 60-second answer ready: "I'm [Name], I recently developed a passion for data analysis. I've spent the last few months building my skills in SQL and Power BI, and I'm excited to apply those skills to solve real business problems.")

- "Why are you interested in this role?"
- "What are your salary expectations?" (Do your research beforehand!)

Stage 2: The Technical Screen

Goal: To verify your technical skills. This can take two forms:

- **A Live SQL Test:** You'll be given a few simple-to-medium difficulty SQL problems to solve in a shared screen environment. They want to see your thought process. *Practice on HackerRank or LeetCode!*
- **A Take-Home Assignment:** You'll be given a dataset and 2-3 days to clean, analyze, and present your findings, usually in a short presentation or dashboard. **Treat this like a mini project for your portfolio.**

Stage 3: The Hiring Manager & Team Interview

Goal: To see if you'd be a good fit for the team and to understand how you think about problems.

Common Questions:

- **"Walk me through a project from your portfolio."** (This is the moment you've been waiting for! Pick your best project and use the "Problem-Process-Insight" structure from your README file to tell a clear, concise story.)

- "Here's a hypothetical business problem... how would you approach it?" (They don't care about the right answer. They care about your thought process. Ask clarifying questions! "What data would we have available? What's the exact definition of 'active user'?")

You are now prepared. You have a strategy for networking, a polished online presence, and a clear understanding of the interview process you are about to face.

10.5 Your Roadmap Checklist

☐ My LinkedIn profile reflects my direction clearly.

☐ My portfolio link is featured.

☐ I have prepared and practiced my 60 second introduction.

☐ I have engaged with professionals in my field.

☐ I understand the three-stage interview structure.

You have all the tools you need to land your first role. But what happens after you get the offer? The first few months on the job can be just as challenging as the interview process.

In the next chapter, we will discuss how to make your first 90 days a resounding success, build strong relationships with your new colleagues, and set yourself up for a long and successful career in the incredible field of data analytics. Let's bring it home.

11

YOUR FIRST 90 DAYS AND BEYOND

Thriving as a Data Analyst

The transition from a data enthusiast building portfolio projects to a professional data analyst is the final, most crucial step on your roadmap. All the technical skills, portfolio projects, and networking you've done have led to this moment.

Your journey as a student is over, and your journey as a professional begins. The first three months of any new job can feel overwhelming. The goal is not to be the smartest person in the room or to know everything on day one. The goal is to be a sponge: to learn, build trust, and set the foundation for a successful career.

I remember my first six months on the job vividly. I was eager to prove myself, armed with all the right technical skills. But I quickly learned that the real challenges weren't in the SQL or Python code.

My first major hurdle was storytelling. I was so focused on the perfect query that my initial reports were dry and filled with dense tables that didn't tell a clear story. I had to redo them multiple times. The lesson was profound: technical skill gets you the data, but storytelling gets you the decision.

Then came the challenge of accountability. I missed a deadline on a critical project, not because I was lazy, but because I failed to communicate the roadblock in advance. I kept quiet, hoping to catch up, and that breakdown of trust was far more damaging than the delay itself. I learned that your manager needs to trust your process more than your speed.

But the real turning point came around the 90-day mark. I was in a meeting, and I stood up and told my manager I wanted more work. I wasn't challenged enough, and I wanted to make a bigger impact. He was pleased and assigned me more complex work. The lesson here is that you must proactively own your growth. Don't wait for permission to be great.

These three lessons, storytelling, accountability, and proactive growth, are the non-technical pillars of your success. This chapter will give you the structured roadmap I wish I had, so you can avoid my mistakes and accelerate your impact.

11.1 The Professional Analyst's 90-Day Plan

A structured approach to your first three months will transform you from a new hire into a valuable team member. This plan is designed to shift your focus from what you know to how you apply that knowledge to drive business value.

11.2 Phase 1: The First 30 Days - Be a Sponge

Your primary focus in the first month is not to write code or build dashboards, but to listen, learn the business, and understand the data ecosystem. Your goal is to map out the company's data flow and the key business questions your team answers.

- **Focus on the Business:** Before you can analyze the data, you must understand the business. What does the company sell? Who are its customers? How does it make money? What do the acronyms everyone use mean? Ask "dumb" questions. Write everything down.

- **Understand the Data:** Schedule time with a senior analyst or your manager. Ask them to walk you through the main databases and tables. What data is collected? Where does it come from? What are the most important tables and columns for your team?

- **Meet Your Key People:** Identify and introduce yourself to two types of colleagues:
    - **Data Producers:** The people who create the data (like software engineers).
    - **Data Consumers:** The people who will use your analysis (like marketers or product managers).

- **Your Goal by Day 30:** To be able to explain, in simple terms, what your team does and how the data flows through the company's systems.

11.3 Phase 2 (Days 31–60): Deliver Your First "Small Win"

By now, you should have enough context to take on a small, contained project. This is your chance to demonstrate competence, build confidence, and prove you can translate business needs into data solutions. Remember the lesson on storytelling; make sure your first deliverable is clear, concise, and focused on business impact.

- **Ask for a "Low-Stakes" Project:** Work with your manager to identify a small, well-defined project. This could be updating an existing dashboard, analyzing the results of a recent marketing email, or documenting a dataset.

- **Focus on Process, Not Perfection:** On your first project, your manager is watching *how* you work. Do you ask for help when you're stuck? Do you communicate your progress? Do you double-check your work before you submit it? The process is more important than a perfect result.

- **Document Everything:** As you work on your project, write down the steps you took, the SQL queries you wrote, and the logic you used. This will be invaluable for you and your team later.

- **Your Goal by Day 60:** To have successfully completed one small project from start to finish, building trust with your manager and your team.

11.4 Phase 3 (Days 61–90): Become a Proactive Contributor

You are no longer the "new person." You are an integrated member of the team. Your focus shifts to taking ownership of your career trajectory and identifying areas where you can drive greater impact. This is where you apply the lesson of proactive growth and start looking for the next challenge.

- **Start to Form Your Own Questions:** As you work with the data, you'll start to notice interesting patterns or things that don't make sense. Start a document called "Curious Questions" and share it with your manager during your one-on-one meetings.

- **Refine an Existing Process:** Find one small, repetitive task your team does and see if you can make it a little bit better. Can you automate a query? Can you improve the design of a chart on a dashboard?

- **Set Your First Professional Goals:** Sit down with your manager and have a conversation about your future. What skills do you want to develop over the next six months? What kinds of projects do you want to work on?

- **Your Goal by Day 90:** To be seen as a reliable, curious, and integrated member of the team who not only completes assigned tasks but also thinks critically about the business.

11.5 The Lifelong Learner: Your Journey Never Ends

The tools and technologies in the data world are constantly changing. The most successful analysts are the ones who remain curious and make learning a lifelong habit.

Now that you have learned how to establish yourself as an impactful analyst, it's time to turn your attention to another cornerstone: data ethics and privacy. Handling data carelessly can undermine trust, damage reputation and even break the law. In the next chapter, we are going to learn how to apply professional discretion when handling data.

11.6 Your Roadmap Checklist

☐ I understand the goals for my first 30, 60, and 90 days.

☐ I commit to communicating proactively.

☐ I will document questions and insights.

☐ I will schedule a growth conversation with my manager.

☐ I will continue learning intentionally.

12

THE RESPONSIBLE ANALYST

Data Ethics and Privacy

As a data analyst, you will be given access to the most sensitive information your company holds. Customer records. Employee data. Financial transactions. Behavioral patterns. This power comes with immense responsibility.

Data ethics and privacy are not abstract academic concepts. They are practical safeguards that protect individuals, the company, and your own professional reputation. A single careless mistake with sensitive information can damage trust in ways that are difficult to repair.

12.1 The Core Principle: Data Represents People

Always remember that every row of data represents a person, a customer, or an employee. Treat that data with the respect and security it deserves. Ethical data use means ensuring your analysis does not lead to unfair, biased, or discriminatory outcomes

Ethical Consideration	Practical Application
Bias	Actively check your data for underrepresented groups. Does your model perform equally well for all demographics?
Fairness	Ensure your analysis is not used to deny opportunities (e.g., loans, job applications) based on protected characteristics.
Transparency	Be clear about the limitations of your data and your analysis. Don't overstate certainty.

12.2 Understanding Data Privacy

You don't need to be a lawyer, but you must know about **PII (Personally Identifiable Information)**—any data that can be used to identify a specific individual (names, emails, addresses, social security numbers, etc.).

Laws like the **General Data Protection Regulation (GDPR)** in Europe and the **California Consumer Privacy Act (CCPA)** in the US govern how this data must be handled. These laws are built on the principle that individuals have a right to know what data is collected about them and to request its deletion.

Your Operational Safeguard: If you are not explicitly told you need PII for your analysis, **do not use it.** Work with anonymized or aggregated data whenever possible.

12.3 Avoiding Accidental Misuse

The most common mistake beginners make is accidentally exposing PII or sensitive company information.

- **The Trap:** You build a great project for your public portfolio (GitHub) and forget to remove the CustomerName or Email column from the dataset you upload.

- **The Fix:** Always **anonymize** or **aggregate** data before sharing it publicly. Replace names with Customer_A, Customer_B, or simply remove the column entirely. Never use real company data in a public portfolio unless it has been explicitly approved by your legal or compliance team.

12.4 Ethical Visualization

Your analysis must be unbiased. Never manipulate a chart's axis to exaggerate a trend or hide a decline.

Unethical Practice	Ethical Solution
Truncating the Y-axis to make a small change look dramatic.	Always start the Y-axis at zero for bar charts and clearly label the axis range for line charts.
Using misleading color palettes (e.g., red for a positive trend).	Use intuitive color schemes (e.g., green for positive, red for negative).
Omitting key context or time periods that contradict your conclusion.	Present the full picture, even if the results are not what the business wants to hear.

Your ethical safeguard: Present the data truthfully, even if the results are not what the business wants to hear. Your integrity is your most valuable asset.

Conclusion

You have reached the end of the roadmap. But it's not really an end, is it? It's the beginning. Think back to the person you were when you first opened this book. You were curious, perhaps a little intimidated, and standing at the bottom of a mountain, unsure of the path.

Now, look at how far you've come. You learned to think like an analyst, to ask the right questions and to be skeptical of easy answers. You mastered the spreadsheet, the universal tool of business. You learned SQL, the language of data, and can now speak directly to massive databases.

You learned the art of data visualization, turning sterile numbers into compelling stories with Power BI and Tableau. You even took your first steps into the world of programming with Python.

Most importantly, you didn't just learn; you *built*. You have a professional portfolio website, showcasing a collection of projects that prove your skills. You have a job-ready resume and the confidence to walk into an interview and tell the story of your work.

You are no longer just a beginner; you are a practitioner. You are a data analyst. The path forward is now yours to forge. The world is filled with fascinating data and unanswered questions. Go answer them. Find insights that no one else has found. Build things that help people make smarter decisions. Never, ever stop being curious.

Your journey as a data analyst begins now.

Appendix: Extended Practice Guides

Throughout this book, we focused on clarity, structure, and direction rather than overwhelming technical depth.

In Chapter 3, you built your spreadsheet foundation and learned structured thinking through Excel.

In Chapter 4, you developed independence by learning how SQL allows you to retrieve and analyze data directly from databases.

In Chapter 7, you structured your professional portfolio with intention and clarity.

If you would like deeper, step-by-step practice in any of these areas, I have created structured companion guides designed to reinforce those exact chapters.

These guides include:

- Expanded walkthroughs and demonstrations
- Practical exercises for hands-on learning
- Structured templates for project documentation

- Implementation frameworks to strengthen execution

They are designed to help you move from understanding concepts to applying them with confidence.

These materials are optional. The roadmap you completed in this book already provides the essential foundation. However, if you prefer additional guided practice or ready-to-use templates, the companion guides are available to support your continued growth.

To access these materials, please refer to the QR code provided on the following page.

Recommended Learning Resources

Your journey does not end with this book. The field of data analytics evolves continuously, and consistent skill refinement is what separates competent analysts from exceptional ones.

If you are looking for structured platforms to deepen your technical expertise, the following learning paths can help reinforce your foundation:

Strengthening Your Core Tools

If you would like structured, guided practice in:

- https://datacamp.pxf.io/RGNPPX
- https://datacamp.pxf.io/2a04e7
- https://datacamp.pxf.io/DyqPyG
- https://datacamp.pxf.io/3JMJqv

You may explore the recommended training platforms linked through the QR code above. These programs provide hands-on exercises and structured curricula that complement the roadmap you completed in this book. These are not mandatory for success. They are simply additional structured environments for learners who prefer guided progression.

Industry Certifications

Certifications can help signal credibility, especially early in your career. While they do not replace skill or experience, they can strengthen your profile when applying for roles.

Consider pursuing certifications such as:

1. https://datacamp.pxf.io/qzBWWq

2. https://datacamp.pxf.io/55xkko

3. https://datacamp.pxf.io/Wy0OYO

Choose certifications strategically. Focus on those that align with the roles and industries you are targeting.

ABOUT THE AUTHOR

Esther C. Anagu is a seasoned data professional and a passionate advocate for clear, accessible education in the data space. With years of hands-on experience delivering high-impact, data-driven insights in the demanding finance and technology industries, she deeply understands the confusion and challenges aspiring analysts face when trying to start and grow their careers.

Driven by a mission to simplify the journey, Esther created her second book, **The Data Analyst Roadmap** to be the practical, step-by-step guide she wished she had when she began. Her teaching approach blends strong analytical skills with crucial business intelligence—empowering readers to not only analyze data but also influence decisions and drive measurable impact.

Esther holds a degree in Accounting and further advanced her expertise in technology by completing a specialized program in Advanced AI and Automation at Nexford University. She has personally trained and supported thousands of learners across Africa and beyond through her content, workshops, and mentorship.

When she's not analyzing data or creating career-transforming learning experiences, Esther is dedicated to building community, sharing resources that help others grow, and exploring new ways technology can uplift everyday lives. She is the author of Landing Your First Job as a Data Professional, an indispensable guide for data enthusiasts.

If you found this book helpful, Esther would love to hear from you. You can connect with her on LinkedIn, follow her latest projects and resources, or subscribe to her newsletter for ongoing guidance on building your data career.

- LinkedIn: Esther Anagu
- TikTok: anaest_in_tech
- Instagram: anaest_in_tech
- Twitter: Starr_Anagxy
- Medium: estheranagu
- YouTube: anaest_in_tech
- Newsletters: Empowering Data Enthusiasts

www.ingramcontent.com/pod-product-compliance
Lightning Source LLC
Chambersburg PA
CBHW050529240926
51846CB00003B/750
* 9 7 8 9 7 8 6 8 2 2 8 5 3 *